PLATFORM PAPERS

QUARTERLY ESSAYS ON THE PERFORMING ARTS FROM CURRENCY HOUSE

No. 41
November 2014

Platform Papers Partners

We acknowledge with gratitude our Partners in continuing support of Platform Papers and its mission to widen understanding of performing arts practice and encourage change when it is needed:

Gillian Appleton
Anita Luca Belgiorno Nettis Foundation
Jane Bridge
Katharine Brisbane, AM
Bryan Brown, AM and Rachel Ward, AM
Elizabeth Butcher, AM
Penny Chapman
Peter Cooke, OAM
Rowena Cowley and Dr Richard Letts, AM
Michael J. Crouch, AO
Ian Enright
Larry Galbraith
Tony Grierson
Gail Hambly
Wayne Harrison, AM
Peter Lee
Roderick H. McGeoch, AO
David Marr
Harold Mitchell, AC, AO
Joanna Murray-Smith
Helen O'Neil
Martin Portus
Geoffrey Rush, AC
Positive Solutions
Peter Rechniewski
Seaborn Broughton Walford Foundation
Augusta Supple
Andrew Upton
Kim Williams, AM
Professor Di Yerbury, AM

To them and to all subscribers and Friends of Currency House we extend our grateful thanks.

Contents

AVAILABILITY Platform Papers, a series of quarterly essays on the performing arts, is published every February, May, August and November, and is available through bookshops, by subscription or online. For details see our website at www.currencyhouse.org.au/

LETTERS Currency House invites readers to submit letters of 400–1000 words in response to the essays. Letters should be emailed to the Editor at info@currencyhouse.org.au or posted to Currency House at PO Box 2270 Strawberry Hills, NSW 2012, Australia. To be considered for the next issue, they must be received by 15 December 2014.

EDUCATION AND THE ARTS: Creativity in the promised new order

MEG UPTON

WITH NAOMI EDWARDS

About the Authors

MEG UPTON is an experienced drama educator, researcher and youth arts worker in both the arts and education sectors. As education manager at the Malthouse Theatre 2000–08 she created a range of programs and projects that connected young people with practising artists in professional arts settings. She has mentored emerging artists and developed industry-based practice for the Theatre Arts Course at Victoria University and is a co-opted member of Platform Youth Theatre, for whom she a consultant. Meg lectures in Drama Education at Deakin University.

As a researcher she has worked extensively in secondary schools and collaborated with teachers, students and theatre companies, investigating the role of live theatre performance in education. From 2009–11 she was a lead research assistant with the University of Melbourne on the ARC Project *TheatreSpace.* She also works as a consultant teacher with the Melbourne Theatre Company, Malthouse, Arena, RealTV and Performing Lines. Her work with Drama Victoria/Drama Australia has involved sustained consultation around shaping the arts curriculum. She is currently completing a PhD at the University of Melbourne entitled *Teaching the Live: the Pedagogy of Performance.*

NAOMI EDWARDS is a theatre and opera director and arts educator. She has directing credits with Opera Australia and all our major companies and teaching institutions, working in both the main stage and education contexts. Her core practice involves making theatre in cross-sector partnerships with the audience for whom it is intended. She was creative director on the ARC-funded research project Vocal Empowerment, at the University of Melbourne, which explored using actor voice training with young people with cochlear implants; and developed *The Sound of Waves*, with Jodie Harris, a cochlear implantee. She recently adapted *La Cenerentola* for Opera Australia's primary schools touring program and adapted and directed *Hamlet* for Sydney Theatre Company's education program. Her production of Actor on a Box *The Loaded Dog* for STC was nominated for a Sydney Theatre Critics award in 2010. In 2012 her production of *Cautionary Tales for Children* for Arena Theatre was nominated for a Helpmann Award.

A qualified secondary teacher, she has worked extensively as a teaching artist, with young people, elderly, disadvantaged and in teacher training. In 2011 she was awarded the Gloria Dawn/Gloria Payten Fellowship and a Mike Walsh Fellowship which allowed her to visit arts organisations in England, Scotland, Japan and USA to research their education and engagement programs.

ACKNOWLEDGEMENTS

Thank you to my colleague and critical friend Naomi Edwards. Thanks also to the Education Team at the Young Vic, London, for hosting me in 2012. Thank you also to Malthouse Theatre, Melbourne Theatre Company, Sydncy Theatre Company, Chris Kohn, Christine Lucas-Pannan, Jill Smith, Margaret Steven, Robin Penty, Margie Moore and Major Performiing Arts Group Education Network, Noel Jordan and all the highly skilled folk I know who work in the often liminal space of education programs in theatre companies.

Meg Upton

A huge thank you to Meg Upton for all her inspirational work on this paper and in the sector. To the teams at the National Theatre in London, the Globe Theatre, Royal Shakespeare Company, Wolf Trap Foundation for Performing Arts, The New Victory Theater, Centre for Arts Education New York and the Lincoln Centre Institute for your time and generosity on my visits in 2012. Thanks to the Gloria Dawn and Gloria Payten Fellowship and the Mike Walsh Fellowship for making this trip possible. To all the teaching artists, arts educators, teachers of the arts, artists with whom I have worked; your inspiration lies in this paper too.

Naomi Edwards

1 Backpacks in the foyer

There's backpacks in the foyer of the theatre today. There they are...tumbled, school crested, fashionably branded, spilling all over, tripping the unsuspecting. Their owners are oblivious to the impact of these bags because they are on a greater adventure. They're inside a darkened auditorium, or a brightly lit rehearsal room, perhaps even staring in awe at a piled-high higgledy-piggledy props and set store. There's backpacks in the foyer today. A lone mobile rings from one of them, forgotten in the crush by its owner on their way to wherever it is they were going. The owner doesn't care. They're on one of those adventures.

This paper is the story of that pile of backpacks and what they symbolise. It is the story of their owners—students and young people—as audience, as artists, both now and of the future. Specifically it is the story of whether, and indeed how, those backpacks and their owners are regarded and valued by the companies playing host to them. It is also the story of the highly skilled education managers and staff who value education and young people yet often struggle with their own standing and status in the arts organisation of which they are part.

Most performing arts companies don't take their education programs anywhere near as seriously as they could. They can perhaps be forgiven for this, given the contradictory political landscape of the recent past. In late 2012, under the then Federal Labor Government, the education sector and the arts industry was gearing up for a new Australian Curriculum that mandated five art forms for all students in all Australian schools from Foundation to Year 10. There were cautious celebrations. Conversely, in 2012, Liberal Country Party Leader Campbell Newman came to power in Queensland in a landslide victory. Among his first actions was to abolish the Queensland Premier's literary awards, and set about culling $20 million from the Queensland arts budget, particularly from youth arts and education programs. In March 2013, Arts Minister Simon Crean launched a new national cultural policy, *Creative Australia*, one that strongly positioned arts education and arts training as being fundamental to this country's future.[1] *Creative Australia* highlighted the importance of policy in mandating a 'universal arts education for lifelong learning and to drive creativity and innovation'. The policy claimed that, 'every student has the opportunity to receive an arts education, creativity in schools is considered as a vital twenty-first century skill to drive innovation and productivity'. There were more cautious celebrations; but by this time the status of arts funding and its smaller sibling, arts education, was confused and under threat.

In the run up to the federal election in late 2013,

it seemed all bets were off. Despite the Australian Curriculum—the Arts content being published on the Australian Curriculum, Assessment and Reporting Authority (ACARA) website in February 2013—the new Education Minister Christopher Pyne announced an independent review of the curriculum.[2] The catch cry of 'back to basics' once again sounded in our ears. That curriculum, as reviewed, is reportedly on the Minister's desk awaiting a final decision and a signature (see postscript). On Friday 22 August 2014, *Arts Hub* reported that *Creative Australia* was 'dead', including the accompanying funding announced by former Arts Minister Simon Crean in 2013.[3]

In August 2014, the Australian Bureau of Statistics (ABS) released its 2014–18 forward work plan which indicated that arts and sport data would disappear from the federally funded component of its statistics collection. According to *The Conversation* one of several online media sources to report the story, without that data 'we are not in a position to say anything meaningful about Australian sport, the arts or the not-for-profit organisations that predominantly deliver programs' and, significantly, data that might help shape policy would no longer exist.[4] Internationally, within the last twelve months UNESCO has placed arts education as number 48 in its list of ongoing priorities. Effectively, this means that UNESCO arts education programs may not exist beyond November this year. Never mind that its *Road Map for Arts Education* (2006) spends three pages clearly stating that young people's right to cultural participation is outlined in the Declaration of Human Rights, and in the Convention on the Rights of the Child.[5] Within this political maelstrom, at state, federal and international level, clear messages are being sent; ones that raise serious questions about whether governments value the arts in education and in the broader community. Why should theatre companies take their education programs seriously if governments, key organisations and peak bodies don't appear to appreciate arts education themselves?

Our experience, derived from over fifteen years in the sector, has indicated that recent shifts at the top in arts organisations place education programs in precarious positions. Every time there is leadership change in a company, or the membership of a board is refreshed, the education program comes under scrutiny and potentially under threat. We certainly don't argue that education programs should be immune from scrutiny. Good art and business practice demands constant reappraisal. But why, as is often the case, when arts organisations meet tough times, are education and community programs the most at risk?

Take, for example, a significant ripple in the universe that occurred in 2012 when Sydney Theatre Company, under the stewardship of its then artistic directors, dismantled the education program along with the incumbent education team. The following year a new education manager was appointed and the invention or reinvention of an education program began but with a vastly different remit. The question is, what were the internal motives behind the restructure? Within the parameters of that change, the high-quality full-scale education productions programmed in response to the curriculum disappeared. Tailor-made workshops of seminal texts also vanished, as did the series of works made specifically for very young children. What was STC responding to? What does the shift from 'education' to 'community' signify?

In 2011, Malthouse Theatre in Melbourne reduced the education manager's role from a fulltime to three days per week. Recently, this has been increased to four days per week; but, again, what changed? What was Malthouse responding to? What shifts had occurred internally? These are key questions for theatre companies. It is a frustrating time and a confusing landscape for arts education. It warrants new initiatives. Young people are, more than ever, reliant on theatre companies for quality arts experiences and arts education.

Waiting on Government

Under the former Labor Government, a first ever national curriculum for students from Foundation Year (Year F) to Year 10 was scoped and ratified by the states. Within the renamed Australian Curriculum, *all students in Years F to 10 have an entitlement to an arts education.* Associate Professor, Sandra Gattenhof, Queensland University of Technology, calls this statement of entitlement an 'historic moment'. She comments,

> *We have a curriculum that provides an entitlement to five art forms for all young Australians. That's never happened before.*[6]

The new curriculum clearly positions students as art makers and audiences of *now,* not of the *future* as they so often have been labelled. Gattenhof believes that this will allow young Australians to engage fully in the arts, and to understand the distinctive capacities of the arts to make meaning. This is powerful positioning and offers a unique opportunity for performing arts companies.

We recognise that excellent work is happening in some Australian theatre companies with regard to education programs. Such work is driven by creative individuals who enable rich cultural experiences for young people. But the arrival of such individuals is often serendipitous and serendipity such as does not make for a sustainable education program. The questions around the existence of education programs, their ongoing development and championing in theatre companies are hot ones. It is a significant driver of this paper. We argue for a paradigm shift, one that places education programs front and centre as *the* model for building vibrant theatre companies. For the authors, the presence of a mass of backpacks in a foyer both sends a powerful signal that something's is going on, and warns that the rhetoric of those in leadership positions needs to fit the emergent reality in terms of the constancy, status, and resourcing of education programs within Australian theatre companies. Further, we argue that performing arts organisations need to circumvent the vacillations of government and policy and assert their responsibility in the delivery of arts education.

In researching and writing this paper we acknowledge ongoing change in the sector and the fluid nature of programs and practice. We draw strongly on our years of practice in the theatre and education space. We draw on our work and research in curriculum and pedagogy. We spoke with education managers, artistic directors and general managers past and present across several theatre companies. We mined the websites and education program statements and annual general reports of many companies, and we attended the recently established Major Performing Arts Groups Education Forum in 2013 and 2014. Over these three years we have sought to gain broad insight into current thinking around, and the positioning of, education programs in major arts organisations.

2. Why do we need education programs in theatre companies?

We were encouraged by a recent phone call from a Melbourne-based theatre company who wanted advice. 'We want to create an education program for our company. Would you be able to attend a strategic planning meeting and offer some insight?' The meeting was energetic and the company posed powerful, searching questions:

What would an education program look like?
How would it fit with the company's current goals and strategies?
How would it work with the new Australian curriculum materials being introduced?
What partnerships could support it, both short term and long term?
What would it need to properly resource it?
How would it fit with our current artist program?
How could it potentially grow?
What opportunities, benefits could it offer a theatre company; young people and their teachers?

> *What would be the terms of engagement?*
> *Would the program be resourced and be sustainable?*
> *How would it innovate?*

A critical question was: *Why?*

> *Why does a theatre company want an education program?*
> *Why would it need an education program?*

Sonia Bahri has written:

> *Art is part of each country's wealth, of each culture's capital. It is our common heritage, the patrimony of all. However, this capital is not always used for transmission of knowledge and for educational purposes. The potential of the arts on students' interests and learning is neglected despite its availability everywhere in the world.*[7]

The transformative potential of arts education has been well established over many years, but particularly the past twenty years, revealed by significant findings from a series of key research projects, longitudinal in their approach, rigorous in their methodology and unequivocal in their reported results. We now know, because research tells us so, that great arts education and powerful arts experiences can transform the lives of young people. They build capacity to journey through life and to contribute to its betterment.

One of the most influential reports on the impact of arts education on young people's lives is *Champions of Change: The Impact of the Arts on Learning* (2000).[8] The report emphatically states that 'When young people are involved with the arts, something changes in their lives.' Rather than marketing the smiling faces of young people watching a performance, *Champions of Change* investigates how the arts change the learning experiences of young people. It concludes that:

> *The arts reach students who are not otherwise being reached.*
> *The arts reach students in ways by which they are not otherwise being reached.*
> *The arts connect students to themselves and each other.*
> *The arts transform the environment for learning*
> *The arts provide learning opportunities for the adults in the lives of young people.*
> *The arts provide new challenges for those students already considered successful.*
> *The arts connect learning experiences to the world of real work.*

Wendy Schiller's study *Children's Voices* indicates how powerful a live performance can be for children.[9] Schiller's research demonstrates that children clearly recognise the links between a live arts performance and their own lives. They show an understanding of the contribution of audience, actors, and directors.

Importantly they develop an improvement in literacy outcomes through their increased motivation to write stories, diaries and plays. Further, they are articulate about what they like and didn't like about what they see; and about how a performance can be improved. In summary, the research found that children's engagement with a live performance is a seminal experience, one that had powerful resonances in their lives, in their learning and in their ongoing view of the world.

In 2010, leading arts educator, Professor Robyn Ewing of the University of Sydney, provided what is arguably the most comprehensive overview yet to be conducted of the power and relevance of the arts in education and its impact on young Australians' lives, *The Arts and Australian Education: Realising Potential.* A key finding of Ewing's research is that,

> *Aesthetic knowledge is central to learning, understanding and enabling in our society. However, providing aesthetic knowledge is difficult for schools and teachers, because it is an experience that engages the brain, body and emotions, all together in a range of symbolic languages and forms.*[10]

We argue that the space for building aesthetic knowledge is the space that performing arts companies need to more seriously occupy.

Subsequent to Ewing's landmark research, two other key Australian projects have emerged. Firstly, *Theatre Space: Accessing the Cultural Conversation*—more recently published as *Young Audiences, Theatre and the Cultural Conversation*[11]—a longitudinal study that explored the theatre-going practices of young people between the ages of 16 and 30 and included 13 key performing arts organisations across Queensland, New South Wales and Victoria.[12] The study examined the role of teachers as cultural mediators, young people's theatre literacy, the aesthetic of a venue, the regard given to young people who attend the venue, and the performance context and content. It confirmed what many arts educators and education managers had long believed and clearly understood—that these were all key factors in student engagement with live performance. The potential confluence of these factors offered rich opportunities for theatre companies to actively participate in the education space, it concluded, particularly so when considering audience development and programming.

In late 2013, the Australia Council-University of Sydney study, *The Role of Arts Education in academic motivation, engagement and achievement*,[13] asked further questions about arts education and participation, academic outcomes, multi-nation contexts, engagement and motivation. It found that arts education plays a significant role in the engagement of young people in their own education, in personal motivation and in academic achievement, affirming much of the earlier research and thereby putting to bed, once and for all, any question around the efficacy of arts education in young people's lives.

The National Assessment Program, Literacy and Numeracy (NAPLAN) website states that NAPLAN tests the sorts of skills that are essential for every child to progress through school and life: reading, writing, spelling and numeracy.[14] We agree that these are vital skills but this statement, with its emphasis on outcomes, flies in the face of the powerful research that demonstrates the impact of the arts on *the process* of student learning, literacy and a young person's capacity 'to progress through school and life'. The narrowness of the NAPLAN definition of learning and progression needs to be challenged.

The MacArthur Foundation's *Connected Learning* model argues that 'the most meaningful and resilient forms of learning happen when a learner has a personal interest or passion that they are pursuing in a context of cultural affinity, social support and shared purpose.'[15] While the model is built upon learning through new technologies and online platforms, we argue that theatre has similar goals. Concepts of cultural affinity, social support and shared purpose are very much the domain of artistic practice and audience development.

In drawing attention to this rich body of research, we seek to show the opportunities awaiting our theatre companies and encourage them to reconsider how they currently value young people in the overall company model and what 'education' means to them.

Defining education programs in the here and now

By way of defining an education program, Arts Victoria provides a useful overview:

> *Arts education programs are defined as those that have a direct relationship between schools and professional arts and community organisations. They involve primary and secondary students in artistic programs, and have a focus on education.*[16]

Most theatre companies, small, medium and major, have such programs or elect to engage with the education sector as defined by Arts Victoria. Indeed, theatre, drama and education have shared some common territory in Australia for many years. The 1970s and 1980s saw a hey-day of touring Theatre-in-Education or TIE teams such as FM Theatre, Woolley Jumpers, and Barnstorm. This tradition is continued by contemporary companies such as—and this is a small list—IS Theatre, Brainstorm Productions, Class Act, KITE, Jigsaw, Imaginary Theatre, Shake & Stir, TIE and The Flying Bookworm. Internationally, the relationship between theatre organisations and education has been captured in several landmark publications.[17] This paper is confined to the question of how Australia's major theatre companies have participated in the education space, historically, currently and as a way of commandeering the leadership in arts education for the future. Major companies have the capacity to present theatre with full production values created using the best available resources and with the best artists. It is crucial that young people have broad access to work of this calibre.

So, how do some of Australia's flagship theatre companies describe their approach to education and the arts? Several company websites provided the following rich insights:

- *Sydney Theatre Company's mission is to provide young people in NSW with possibilities to play, imagine and learn through the provision of theatre and theatre-based education programs of the highest standard'*—Sydney Theatre Company, 2014.
- *Young people are all artists in the sense that they are constantly questioning the new world that they are becoming accustomed to. We believe that theatre is a powerful medium that connects us all to our inner child*—State Theatre Company of South Australia, 2014.
- *Each year, MTC's Education Program shines the light for thousands of young people through … access to world-class productions and learning programs. We believe in giving young people the opportunity to experience exceptional theatre, and we hope this will inspire a passion that will last a lifetime*—Melbourne Theatre Company, 2014.
- *We inspire and educate young people through school performances, workshops, and teacher*

training. We support the industry by creating new work, and providing early-career artists with paid opportunities to develop their talents—Queensland Theatre Company, 2014.

- *At Bell Shakespeare, education is at the heart of everything we do*—Bell Shakespeare, 2014.
- *Throughout the year, we offer opportunities for Tasmanians of all ages to participate in, learn about and create theatre, enriching Tasmania as a place to live*—Tasmanian Theatre Company, 2014.[18]

Four other major Australian theatre companies' approaches to education are also worth considering:

- *Black Swan is committed to supporting educators in developing an appreciation of the Performing Arts. Our mission is to be accessible to all school communities with selected performances, workshops, quality resources and value adding experiences that support and complement the West Australian and Australian Curriculum*—Black Swan Theatre Company, Perth.
- *Our Education Program provides students and teachers with insights into the work of Belvoir and first hand experiences of the theatre-making process. We believe that Belvoir's body of work has as much to offer a schools audience as it does an adult audience and our Education program aims to support all*

students in experiencing and understanding our work.—Belvoir Theatre, Sydney.

- *We offer both pre-programmed workshops and activities, as well as boutique and bespoke experiences adapted to your individual needs as a teacher. This varied combination of inspiration, education and provocation teaches radical theatre*—Malthouse Theatre, Melbourne
- *We are thrilled to bring you the education highlights of our 2014 season… Here is joyous comedy, high adventure, twists on the familiar and turns of the unexpected. At the same time, we know you are looking for … theatre with substance, shows with real syllabus connections, support materials and texts worth sharing with students*—La Boite, Brisbane.

The emotive nature of this language reveals a high level of aspiration on the part of the theatre companies. Throughout the country, theatre companies state that they offer students and young people the opportunity to: play, imagine, learn, be an artist, experience exceptional live theatre, have high quality learning experiences, participate, create, appreciate, have access to, have insight into, understand, be provoked. Further, they provide teachers with syllabus connections, the promise of rich resources and early-career artists with paid opportunities to develop their talents. These prospects are exciting and suggest huge potential for young people's learning and lived experience.

Deeper investigation reveals a range of specific ways about *how* each company intends to achieve these aims: through participatory programs such as workshops, creative response projects, outreach, work experience, and ambassadorial programs; and through subsidised attendance and more curriculum or syllabus-centred approaches such as workshops, tours, forums and resources.

The offerings across companies are not dissimilar but variations arise when companies choose to develop and program work specifically for schools' and/or young audiences; tour *into* schools; or invite young people to create and perform their own responses to project proposals. For example, Sydney Theatre Company's recently developed 'School Drama', in collaboration with the University of Sydney, a school-based program that uses teaching artists and drama pedagogy as a means of building young people's literacy. Malthouse Theatre's 'Suitcase Series' invites students in years nine and ten to make a creative response to issues around sustainability and then perform it in the theatre, working alongside an ensemble of professional artists. Queensland Theatre Company's 'The Scene Project' is somewhat similar, and Bell Shakespeare has a long tradition of connecting students to Shakespeare through their in-schools 'Actors-at-Work' program.

So, is there anything actually wrong here? On the surface, no, but on closer scrutiny cracks begin to emerge.

3. Education: What does it even mean?

The term 'education' attracts tension for a variety of reasons. The discourse around education in recent times has been one of economics and productivity. The schools website page of the Federal Department of Education states that:

> *High quality school education supports productivity and improves the educational outcomes of children, increasing the likelihood that they will attain skills and be in employment.*[19]

Like the limitations of NAPLAN's claim for the unquestioned dominance of literacy and numeracy, this is a reductive description of education and arguably diminishes the potential learning experiences for young Australians. We feel there is much to challenge within it and that there is good reason why a theatre company might want to distance itself from such a view. Despite the rich accounts of education programs on theatre company websites, however, there appears to be no shared sector understanding of what the term 'education' actually means.

A symptom of this unease and uncertainty can be seen in the titles of the current education programs being offered on their sites. While some of the profiled companies, listed earlier, position their programs clearly as 'Education', others distance themselves from the term. QTC has added 'Youth' to its banner. Bell Shakespeare is about 'Learning'. Others are embedded in other titles or drop downs. You can find the education programs of STC and TTC under 'Community'; Malthouse has become crafty and re-named their program 'Prompt' (although it is still housed under Education). Internationally, arts and cultural organisations have purposefully renamed or re-branded their education programs with such titles as *Discovery, Participation, Young Audience, Explore, Enrichment, Engagement* and *Backstage*. Each title conjures a different prospect. The UK's National Theatre, for instance, has, under 'Learning', separated 'Schools & Teachers' from 'Young People', an interesting and telling distinction.

Asked what she thought about the word 'education' in her job description, education manager at Melbourne Theatre Company, Suzie Thomas admitted it was 'something we've struggled with. You want it to say what it is but it is more than that…'—It could be a dirty word in the context of a theatre company. 'I think that many sectors have a problem with the word 'education' and for some it worries them…but what would we replace it with? We don't want it to be a political word or something naff.' The term 'education' suggested that a company's engagement in community is with schools, students and teachers only and there is resistance to this. As Thomas says, 'it's more than that'.

Artistic director of MTC Brett Sheehy concurred, commenting that the term 'education' was 'a bit dry and dutiful rather than playful', a more playful experience being one he hoped MTC could offer its audiences.

Melbourne Theatre Company is not the only company struggling with the associations of the term 'education'. Associate producer Josh Wright of Malthouse Theatre commented that the company made a conscious choice to choose a name for their program that placed education 'in a wider context and [helped] to understand it as a starting point or an enhancing point'. They called it 'Prompt'. According to Wright, Prompt is closely linked to the creative aims of Malthouse Theatre in that it suggests 'an ongoing conversation…provoking you to continue your own investigation'. Youth and education manager Clare Watson agreed.[20] She felt that calling their education program 'Prompt' was concerned with 'moving away from the criteria-based system that is the education system', and letting their program 'sit outside that and respond to the work, the artists involved and the students' interests'.

There are other tensions associated with using the term 'education' for a theatre company program. Former head of participation at Arts Centre Melbourne, Robin Penty, stated that the term 'education' could draw a demarcation around audiences or types of audience. From our experience we believe there is currency to such demarcation and clear evidence that the term 'education' is commonly used to define types of audiences. For example, QTC and STC offer specific 'schools' days for some of their main stage performances, Barking Gecko identifies certain shows as 'available for school excursions' and Bell Shakespeare produces an in-theatre touring production each year for schools' audiences only. The practice of programming schools performances suggests that within each company someone has decided what an education or schools audience is, when they should come and what they will see. But who will decide? At best this is a problematic practice. If matinees and 'school days' are offered in the main stage seasons, then what is being developed or curated with education in mind?

The case of *Moth*

In the context of this paper's focus on education and theatre companies, Declan Greene's *Moth* is a powerful example of boundary blurring:[21] that is, the blurring of the distinction between what, in a theatre company's mind, constitutes performance for an education audience and performance for an adult audience. *Moth* provides an example of theatre companies and teachers needing to know each other's territory more thoroughly. Commissioned by Chris Kohn, then artistic director of Melbourne's Arena Theatre Company,[22] *Moth* was co-produced with Malthouse Theatre and then toured nationally. It is a challenging and provocative story, non-naturalistic in stage style, about two marginalised

16-year-olds, and includes representations of mental illness, religious visitations, risk-taking behaviour, assault and imperfect friendship. The adults in the play are depicted through the lens of the two young characters.

At the Drama Victoria Conference in 2010, Kohn and Meg Upton co-presented a session entitled 'Challenging theatre for young people'. During the presentation, Kohn drew attention to Arena Theatre Company's process of creating risky work. Arena begins with rigorous research. They then directly engage with the intended audience throughout the development process, including having groups of young people in the rehearsal room. Then the research and audience are set aside for a while, to 'allow ourselves to freely follow our artistic impulses'. Finally, Kohn explained, the developing work is 'reunited' with the research and the intended audience. 'This is an ongoing process from the first brainstorm to the opening night', he said.[23] In more detail, Kohn described a moment in the development of the work where the main character, Sebastian, faces death in a manner that could be interpreted as suicide, or as a provocation for police to shoot him. The danger was that suicide might be seen as being 'cool' and there was 'no way' that Arena wanted that to happen. They presented a number of options to the young people present including a scene in which Sebastian complied with police requests and another where he was shot but survived. These ideas were apparently 'shouted down' by the students who insisted that Sebastian had to die and that any other version would 'water down the tragedy' and would 'betray their emotional investment in the characters'. Kohn stated,

> *In the end, we found a way, I believe, to depict the tragedy of his death without glamorising the act, and, crucially, within the dramaturgy, depict Sebastian's regret for what happened, make it clear that he was in the grips of a delusion and not making rational decisions, and demonstrating the impact his death had on a friend he left behind.*

Declan Greene's *Moth* was shortlisted for a Victorian Premier's Literary Award in 2010. In the same year it won the Malcolm Robertson Prize, and the Green Room award for best new writing for Australian theatre. In 2011 the play won an AWGIE for outstanding writing for young audiences. These are significant accolades, yet the work remained 'problematic' for some. The content of *Moth* traversed traditional audience demarcation lines for educators and for performance venues. In the intended authenticity of the work lay its danger. For two years, *Moth* was unsuccessful in its application to the Victorian Playlists, being considered too risky and challenging for even senior secondary students. Without the support of the curriculum, venues were dubious about who the audience for such a work would be. *Moth* didn't fit snugly into any box.

4. Audience development

Audiences, audience development, and audience retention are recognised as key drivers in theatre companies' programming, marketing and promotion. But what is the direct relationship between audiences, audience development and education programs? The Australia Council for the Arts, *Anticipating Change in the Major Performing Arts* report (2008) states that a number of Major Performing Arts companies have developed school programs to 'build connections with audiences of the future'.[24] Anyone who has sat in a theatre with an audience comprising large groups of students and young people knows that they are not audiences of the future they are audiences of *now*: digitally savvy complex thinkers, media consumers and art makers. They go to school but school is not their only go-to place.

The 2010 Australia Council report, *More than Bums on Seats,* sought to show that many Australians—including young people—are not just consumers of the arts but also engaged participants.[25] Despite this we feel that some major theatre companies still regard students as no more than bums-on-seats. As an education manager, Meg recalls being asked on several occasions when a show was not selling well to 'find' a schools' audience. Conversely, when a show was selling well, significant constraints would be placed around school audience access. The argument that connecting with the education sector will build audiences and fill theatres, is limiting and can be contradictory. Such thinking pays little regard to the young people themselves and the cultural experiences they want to have, or will have. In recent years research has well established that audiences have more to offer. Radbourne, Glow, Johansson and White's research supports the notion that '[adult] audiences are active participants and that they seek out work that increases their knowledge, provides risk, is authentic and offers collective engagement'.[26] Young people are no different. *Theatre Space* raises this very point.[27] As research, it traverses the territory of how young people are invited into theatre companies, how their presence in the theatre building is regarded, and how this is as critical to their experience as it is for adult audiences. It confirms what the authors, as practitioners, deeply know. For a theatre company, *why* you want students in the building or in your theatre, and *how* they will be regarded when present, requires serious contemplation. The following example throws this idea into sharp relief.

An awkward pause

> *The year is 2004 and Martin Flanagan's* The Call, *a theatrical rendering of Tom Wills and the beginnings of Australian Rules Football, is playing in the Beckett Theatre at Playbox Theatre*

> *Company. As part of the Melbourne International Arts Festival, it attracts several groups of students. On this particular day, a matinee, the students in the audience are lively and vocal. They are also seated in the first few rows of the auditorium. What happened afterwards was somewhat surprising. The cast complained to management about the students' behaviour and in an awkward meeting between all, the education staff faced an emotional barrage. The students' behaviour was interpreted as disrespectful. Further, the cast might not be willing to have students in the theatre again if 'we'—meaning the education staff—couldn't guarantee their behaviour. It was somewhat breathtaking. Particularly when you consider whether there would ever be a meeting called between staff and management about adult behaviour in the theatre auditorium.*[28]

The anecdote serves to illustrate how young audiences can be seen within a company. The school bookings were welcome because they did indeed provide bums-on-seats, but what that might really mean in practice wasn't a matter given adequate consideration.

A further cautionary tale. From 2002 to 2005, Ilbijerri Aboriginal and Torres Strait Islander Theatre and Playbox Theatre Company co-produced Jane Harrison's play *Stolen,* a play exploring the forced removal of Indigenous children from their families, for VCE English students in Victoria. Staged in the

Merlyn Theatre at the CUB Malthouse the cast played almost exclusively to student audiences of over 350 per performance. Many students had never attended a live theatre performance before. Every time the lights went down there was the familiar whistling, cheering, and 'in the dark' noise. In that first season in 2002, the safety-in-the-dark anonymity people believe they have on social media or in a crowd at the football spilled over into racial slurs and other behaviours that were deeply disturbing and upsetting for the cast and creative team. As an organisation Playbox Theatre Company was confronted with a vacuum in its production process. It was a great thing to sell 350 tickets to each show. It was another to consider the social and educational impact of that transaction on particular groups of ticketholders.

Strident conversations were held and structured protocols developed before the 2003 season and the conversations and protocols were as much cultural and pedagogical as organisational. It was a critical moment for the education program. Such discussion enabled education staff to consistently and effectively communicate with casts and creative teams prior to the attendance of school audiences, and therefore, establish what the presence of school groups in the audience might mean. Further, it recognised the ongoing need to communicate effectively with teachers and schools and the vigilance required by the education team to achieve the best possible experience for the students and the performers. One former education manager observed that in her experience a theatre company should continually ask itself how it felt about having 'lots of kids in the building' and whether the artists would complain that they didn't train to be an actor to play to 'a theatre load of ungrateful kids!' Even the notion that an audience should be 'grateful' raises interesting issues.

The point that both these incidents raise is that a theatre company, collectively and collaboratively, must consider what it means to engage with the education sector as an audience-building activity, but also in a deeper and more meaningful way.

5. Theatre and the changing curriculum

> *Arts education is critical to future arts participation and public valuation of the arts, and an important part of a balanced education. Efforts are underway to establish a unified, comprehensive arts education policy on a national level, which, if implemented, would vastly improve the general educational offer and may offer MPA companies opportunities to have greater efficacy in reaching and teaching children. Currently, however, arts education guidelines and curricula are developed piecemeal on a state by state, and often school by school, basis.*[29]

The coming Australian Curriculum is a critical part of this discussion. Education programs within theatre companies have historically been tied to state-based curricula and syllabi. Providing clear links between the performed work, or even a workshop program, and state-based curricula is an imperative for theatre companies and many have become savvy about including curriculum or syllabus tables in their education resources that enable teachers to tick boxes within their schools' learning programs.

Both the Melbourne Theatre Company and the Playbox Theatre Company education programs, complete with newly installed education managers, emerged in the early 1990s directly in response to the Victorian curriculum, particularly the development of the new senior Victorian Certificate of Education (VCE). Under the management of Robert McDonald, MTC's education program responded initially to English and Literature curricula, building programs around classic texts, offering cut-down versions for students to have a 'taste', and providing accompanying education resources. Playbox Theatre Company developed a program directly out of the requirements of the Drama and Theatre Studies Designs, offering workshops in play building, monologue, stagecraft and generating education resources for productions that had been selected for the VCE Playlists.

Current MTC education manager, Suzie Thomas observes:

> *Attracting that audience is difficult unless the work is on the curriculum. To put a show on and just expect there to be the time and the money for schools to attend is difficult, so we do need to align the work so the students have that experience... I think a lot when I am programming about the curriculum. It does help us to align certain things in terms of getting to the audience we want.*

The following extract from a Playbox Theatre Company/Malthouse management memo in 2005 clearly outlines the case for aligning aspects of the program to the curriculum, as well as highlighting the critical knowledge that education program staff need to have.

> *The workshop program is essentially what maintains a connection between the Victorian curriculum and Malthouse Education and allows us to speak the same language to schools, students and the VCAA. Many schools book with us because of the breadth of what we offer and because we have insight into and knowledge of what the curriculum requires and what the curriculum dictates in terms of the choices that schools make.*[30]

The difficulties in attracting a schools audience have generated certain practices in the sector. It would be fair to say that many theatre companies have unashamedly mined curriculum text lists over the years and programmed work with the clear intent of attracting schools' audiences. Both the authors of this paper have been complicit in that practice. Classic texts continue to be programmed, more often now as adaptations or radical re-imaginings. At the time of writing this paper, three major productions of *Macbeth* had been or were to be performed around Australia—at QTC, at STC and one touring with Bell Shakespeare. In recent years, major theatre companies around Australia have programmed some of what are arguably the canonical plays of the Western European theatre tradition, including *The Crucible, Rosencrantz and Guildenstern are Dead, Hedda Gabler, The Wild Duck, The Cherry Orchard, The Maids, Death of a Salesman, Romeo and Juliet, The Threepenny Opera, The Government Inspector, Hamlet, Richard III,* and *Mother Courage and her Children*. Our research indicates that many of these productions were heavily subscribed by schools. Is the programming of classic texts antiquated? No, says MTC's Suzie Thomas, 'Some students will go through their entire schooling life not seeing a play performed. So it is important to stage such works.' Perhaps the mining of curriculum text lists provides unintentional opportunities for young people to have their first theatre experience. Perhaps this is better than never experiencing theatre at all.

There is shrewd understanding in the industry that when programmed works align with text lists or learning programs in schools, ticket sales significantly increase. In the example already given, Jane Harrison's *Stolen* appeared on the VCE English text list in Victoria from 2002–2005, generating performances attended by over 20,000 students.[31] Similarly, productions that are listed on the VCE Drama and Theatre Studies Playlists provide significant opportunities for theatre companies. In 2001 Playbox Theatre Company programmed *Svetlana in Slingbacks* by Valentina Levkowicz. It sold 170 student tickets. The same play, remounted for 2002 as part of the VCE curriculum, sold nearly 2,200 student tickets.[32] Malthouse Theatre staff acknowledge that the curriculum is a strong audience development tool, and when a programmed work is selected for the Playlists, young people comprise 25–30% of their audience. They consider actively seeking to have programmed works selected for the Playlists as entrepreneurial and a potential marketing tool. Further, they see the link between their programmed works and the curriculum as both an engagement and diversity strategy: the presence of a broad range of young audiences in the theatre broadens concepts of *who* is in the audience.

Senior Drama curricula differ across Australia. Several states set lists of plays, both from Australian and international contexts, for schools to select from for study purposes. Theatre companies often respond by programming and producing a listed work. Matt Cameron's *Ruby Moon* is a case in point. It has appeared on set script or performance lists and been produced regularly in Victoria, New South Wales, Queensland, and Western Australia in the past five years.

In Victoria studying plays in performance at senior level generates a complex partnership between industry and education sectors. The process involves theatre companies and independent producers applying to the curriculum authority to have their work selected. Applicants supply scripts, an outline of their creative process and any available visual material. Importantly, the selection process requires the theatre company to respond to a series of questions that ask how the production/s will address specific learning areas of the Drama or Theatre Studies curricula.[33] These questions contain a number of embedded assumptions: that theatre companies will be able to interpret the language of the curriculum in order to frame the play, and that the selection panel will be conversant with script reading, contemporary theatre making practice and its language. Such a process directly highlights the need for ongoing cross-sector understanding and knowledge.

These assumptions are not always justified; and any deficiency on the part of the theatre must result, we believe, in problems with the practice of theatre companies dipping opportunistically into the curriculum text lists or inappropriately seeking selection for their play to a curriculum list. Such problems arise when the company appears to view the curriculum merely as a means of building attendance or providing financial viability; and this sidelines or ignores the quality of the students' experience. In the past, as theatre/education mediators we have been approached by producers wanting advice about how to have a play selected to the curriculum to 'guarantee' a season or increase their ticket sales. This approach diminishes the contribution of young people and trivialises the important role that theatre can have in interrogating enduring ideas, and being a point of 'connectivity' to self and others.

6. Curriculum and education disjunctions

Selecting conventionally-interpreted classic texts for programming is not necessarily a silly idea. Classics are known, they are published, and they come with a literary stamp of approval. They offer little challenge to the gatekeepers of the curriculum and to individual school policy. By contrast the programming of new work or radical re-imaginings of classic texts can be risky when the interpretation butts up against education paradigms and perceived community standards. The earlier example of *Moth* provides some insight into the way new work can find itself on the outer with schools' audiences. Chris Kohn, who directed Declan Greene's play, strongly defended both the play and Arena's creative process. 'I feel that we were able to tackle risky, complex and provocative material with due respect and rigour. To set aside such material would be shirking our responsibilities as makers of theatre for young people. But to tackle such material irresponsibly or lazily would be worse.'

Significant research with regard to adolescence suggests that the arts are a powerful way for young people to explore risk but meet the need for a safe and supported environment. The research of Johanna Wyn examines how we consider youth and what it means to be young in the twenty-first century.[34] Jane Kroger states that 'adolescences seem to be a time, at least in many technologically advanced western cultures, when one is confronted with the problem of self-definition'.[35] Phyllis Magrab argues that a key developmental task of adolescence is exploring feelings and allowing adolescents to address those feelings in order to cope with human interaction. She comments:

> *Viewing works of art [in this case THEATRE] allows for the projection of these feelings and provides an opportunity to understand these feelings in a safe environment ... Importantly, the aesthetic experience speaks to developing resiliency in adolescents and promotes youth engagement in learning.*[36]

Melbourne Theatre Company's Suzie Thomas believes that:

> *There is a demand out there for quality and challenging theatre for young people. The greater the level of challenge in the work [...] the greater the level of engagement. The worst thing you can do is condescend or present something boring. Stepping into the risky area is the right way to go'.*[37]

2013 offered two examples of theatre work that tested

notions of 'risk' and 'challenge'. Both cases were in Victoria: *I Love you Bro* by Melbourne writer Adam Cass and *Dance of Death* by August Strindberg in a new version by Tom Holloway. The first play, *I Love you Bro,* 'a tale of love and deceit in a digital world'[38] was programmed for MTC Education and was submitted for VCE Playlist selection but was not chosen because of the subject matter. The second play, *Dance of Death* programmed by Malthouse Theatre was selected but subsequently removed after the adapted version was submitted, again because of the content. The fallout from these two choices is worth some attention.

When he heard that *I Love you Bro* had not been selected, a disappointed Brett Sheehy, MTC artistic director, exclaimed that seventeen-year-olds were only one year under a cinema rating of R; and that what they could view in that category was 'astonishing'. He felt 'deeply disappointed' that 'in the second decade of the twenty-first century in a country like Australia such a decision has been made about work that is so utterly relevant to young people'.

A decision like this draws attention to how the curriculum can become a framing device for many young people's theatre experiences. For MTC's Suzie Thomas the curriculum is an opportunity to engage students as 'critical thinkers' to help them 'understand the world'. She believes that students need to be trusted to think in that way, as do teachers.

The team at Malthouse Theatre were disappointed by the removal of *Dance of Death* from the curriculum playlist. Malthouse Theatre knew the subject matter was risky but had given the script to teachers to read and believed it had a highly experienced education team and creative team, and a responsible plan that included carefully identifying content and maintaining transparency. It had already pre-sold over 800 tickets to schools and had further bookings. The team believed they had implemented their plan in support of the play. But in March/April they were notified that it had been removed. It was felt that the decision-makers had not considered how contemporary theatre was made or the way written language (a play script) was adapted for theatrical production. Malthouse Theatre felt the choice to study and attend *Dance of Death* should lie with the relevant teachers and parents; that it was they who should assess the suitability for the students.[39]

Curriculum authorities are under no obligation to select a particular work from what is on offer at theatre companies. They are accountable at many levels for texts that are set for study and the curriculum has to cater for a diverse range of education contexts and goals. That is not in question. It is, however, impossible to cater for all. The English and Literature text lists across all states include highly challenging novels, films and plays for study but in the end all texts are recommendations only, open to choice.

These are not just cautionary tales about the financial viability of education programs—that is not the concern of the school authorities; instead they reveal certain disjunctions between the assumptions and values of contemporary theatre practice and the requirements of curriculum. *I love you Bro, Dance of Death* and *Moth* highlight the double-edged sword that live theatre offers: exciting live encounters but work in progress, unmediated. The mediation has to occur before and after the event. We must learn to trust young people's capacity to confront challenging material, to be able to position themselves in relation to it and find a response if a safe and supported environment is provided. It is here that education programs provide critical points of intersection.

7. Inside the companies

So far this paper has endeavoured to paint a picture of what education programs within a theatre company might ideally look like, what the historical purposes for their existence are, and how the state-based curricula critically impact on programming and projects. But what is really happening inside theatre companies? What are the opportunities and challenges facing education programs today?

Confessions in the foyer

The emergence of the annual Major Performing Arts Group (MPAG) Education Managers' Forum heralds a significant recognition of education programs in arts and cultural organisations.[40] The recent forum at the Queensland Theatre Company in Brisbane, 2014, provided rich opportunities to network, and share and celebrate best practice amongst the major performing arts organisations. The meeting gathered a large cohort of theatre education managers and other theatre company staff such as general managers and even CEOs. They had two key things in common: a passion for the arts, and a passion for young people. Many of the education managers were young themselves—under 30—but it was on the whole an inter-generational gathering.

One might think that an annual national education forum would signal that all was well and, yes, we knew of rich and valuable work going on in education programs in theatre companies. The Forum, however, provided further insights, particularly in the more informal moments that occurred at lunch or in post-session drinks where different thoughts were articulated ,and a different pattern emerged. Education programs, and those who staff them, often feel marginalised. Many see their positions and the program itself as still requiring an act of internal advocacy. The Forum also revealed a high turnover among education managers. Low wages and the ongoing frustration of justifying their program to artistic directors, management, marketing, philanthropy and boards were the main causes cited. Having been in the game now since 2000, the Forum provided anecdotal evidence for the authors that education program staff still need to rigorously defend their role, while feeling ancillary to the organisation that employs them.

We spoke with Noel Jordan about this paradox. He is a key player in the theatre education space. His professional career includes performing, directing work for young audiences, and programming for young audiences at the Sydney Opera House, Casula and the South Australian Festival *Come Out*. He believes that a certain rhetoric has grown up around young people and young audiences in the arts sector. Cultural organisations 'are very proud of strutting [education programs] out at any kind of photo opportunity' but he believes that funding spent on them and programming for young audiences is 'minimal' in comparison to adult programming.

It is an old argument. Meg recalls 2005 when Playbox Theatre Company was about to become Malthouse. The education team, of which she was a member, felt nervous. Structural change can be powerful, but we were worried. The team put together a pitch to the new leadership. This emphasised the need for the education program 'to work with and journey with the new artistic vision'. We saw the journey as 'pivotal to structuring the program beyond just addressing the curriculum'. In order to do this effectively we believed it would be worthwhile to contribute to the programming process, to transcend reactive practices and plan more effectively.[41]

The pitch made the point that young audiences are great for the company, that education works in partnership with schools to ensure that students come prepared for the experience and that programming and policy with regard to young people and audiences are highly interrelated. The team directly asked the company what value the company placed on young people, what role young people played as part of the company's philosophy, as a box office function—just bums on seats? Further we wanted to write a company Youth Policy that clearly articulated that value. The response was there was no need for a company youth policy because the whole company vision was inclusive of young people. Do theatre companies need dedicated youth policies and education mission statements? Will such policy strengthen the positioning of education programs? We argue yes. Elsewhere in this paper we have highlighted several companies' visions for their education program, and drawn attention to the significance of cultural and education policy disappearing. Policies and mission statements are powerful symbols of intentions and of values, and they provide strong leverage for education staff within their own company.

8. Shifting the paradigm: Building vibrant and sustainable education programs

Creative Australia states that all young Australians deserve an arts education. It frames a commitment to 'a universal arts education for lifelong learning and to drive creativity and innovation.'[42]

Despite *Creative Australia* having been laid to rest by the current government, the leading policy makers in the country certainly believed at one point that arts education was important to young people's education and critical in driving innovation in Australia. It is! And in the absence of government policy we need others to take action. What can this paper offer theatre companies their staff, boards and trustees? What can it provoke in the minds of funding bodies and philanthropic funds? What considerations might it provide for educators? For curriculum writers? Where policy has failed through changed government and vision, theatre companies in partnership with the education sector are well placed to fill the void and we offer the following ways forward, firstly from an organisational perspective and then by re-claiming the term 'education' for innovation.

1. Change values and attitudes

The organisations that have transformed themselves, whether they are theatre companies or other cultural organisations, are those that have moved the young people as participants to the centre of the vision and mission and then transformed the business model and built revenue around that. For those people within the organisation who need to care about that—the finance department, the CEO and the Board—that is a good outcome.

Britain and the United States have admirable models that offer insight into new organisational possibilities. Here are a few examples. The Young Vic Theatre in London has a team of eight in its education program. The company is now 44 years old and its present education program is the result of 'shutting down everything they had once done and starting from scratch'.[43] Having spent years promoting their work to the local community, Sue Emmas, associate artistic director of the Young Vic, conducted a large research project to find out what the community now wanted from them. The result was *Taking Part*. *Taking Part* responded to community feedback, feedback that indicated the community wanted Young Vic to offer engagement in a number of ways; engagement for young people still at school, for young people wanting to participate outside of their schools experience, and for members of the broader local community of whatever age. Young people who reside or go to school in the two boroughs of Southwark and Lambeth which immediately surround the Young Vic, can access the education and performance program for free or for a highly subsidised cost. It is a powerful statement about the regard the Company has and the value they place on the community in which it is situated.

The UK's National Theatre has a team of nineteen across six key learning areas from young children to adult learning. Learning and education are at the core of the National's principles as an arts organisation and of its day-to-day programming practice. While a gallery, the Tate Modern also takes 'a holistic approach that includes how we go about our work, the programs we make and the *experience of participants*'.[44] The conclusion the authors drew from engaging in lengthy conversations with key members of both these organisations is that it was their top-down values and philosophy, their belief that engagement is about life-long learning that was their chief motivation. But they also *acted* on that philosophy in a real way. Some may say this can only be the case with well-funded organisations with powerful remits. This is true, but values and the act of valuing are free and exist beyond any particular company's practice.

Back home, staff from Malthouse Theatre take the view that providing an education program is part of the Company's remit, but to call a program an 'Education Program' undermines the Company's belief that life-long learning and responding to the world is all about education. Calling something a discrete education program doesn't fit well with Malthouse nor does it fit well with the current trends of how education and learning take place. They believe it isn't relevant. We concur, but are curious about whether these views are shared by the whole company, and by whole other companies—it is difficult to tell. What is important is to argue for the rhetoric as it appears on the company website, to clearly and honestly match the reality and practice of the theatre company. Otherwise it is only propaganda.

Embedded in the new Australian Curriculum, the Arts are key values and statements of how arts education contributes to the development of imagination, creativity, human potential, knowledge of self, knowledge of community, knowledge of the world, confidence, and the creation of informed citizens.[45] There is really nothing not to like about these values. Ideally, theatre companies everywhere should be clamouring to uphold them and engage meaningfully with the education sector to assist in delivering these outcomes.

Education programs must be championed by strong artistic leaders who are adaptive, who *value* education and participation, and who actively enable it. There certainly are such leaders out there but, as we have noted, their arrival in a theatre company is often fortuitous and not consistent with any recognised or shared vision within the broader sector. We argue that in the current arts leadership model, education programs have to keep 'pitching', education managers have to keep translating, and the wheel keeps being reinvented. We need cultural change that is not beholden to the individuals who occupy particular positions at given times. Education programs are a significant component of the arts and theatre sector, and the creative industries and *directly* contribute to a company's policy and vision.

Cultural change is required beyond artistic leadership. Our experience has been that the performers, directors and designers in some major theatre companies see the education work they do as a means of getting a leg up into the 'real' work or, as one theatre company states, that part of their education program is to provide 'early-career artists with paid opportunities to develop their talents'. Young people deserve the very best artists and the very best arts experiences. This is not to diminish the work of young artists delivering these educational programs, but nor should we patronise young people by considering work created for them as being a 'leg up', a good opportunity for artists until the 'real work' comes along.

Valuing the presence and contribution of the education program to the theatre company is also important for board members and trustees. They bring particular goals and perspectives to their governance role. An interviewee for this paper commented that a key member of the board of her organisation was sceptical of both the company's education programs and the education system, impacting deeply on the board's decision-making processes. A tension between vision, mission, values and practice is readily apparent and it is a company's responsibility to apply that vision in a top-down approach.

2. Acknowledge the research

The research referenced in this paper is compelling. It is a significant but small part of an enormous body of work that unequivocally demonstrates the power, potential and impact of quality arts education on young people. We urge all stakeholders to read it.

3. Commit resources to evaluate and measure the vibrancy of education programs

Conversations with education managers during the writing of this paper indicated how often they are called upon to provide quantitative and qualitative evidence for marketing, philanthropy and development staff and for funding applications and grant writing. Where does this data come from? How is it collected? What does it actually measure or evaluate? Jennifer Radbourne, Hilary Glow and Katya Johanson discovered that while many artistic directors and general managers could discuss their audience's demographic. 'they knew strangely little about what audiences were getting out of the experience'.[46] These authors argue for research and evaluation that addresses the question: 'What are audiences thinking, feeling and doing as a product of their engagement with arts practices?' There is much more to do than simply collecting statistics about how many young people engaged with the company. We urge theatre companies to adopt a whole of organisation approach to evaluate and measure the vibrancy of their education program, bringing marketing, philanthropy and development into partnership with education to ask urgent questions and seek critical answers from young people, teachers, and the artists with whose work they intersect.

4. Position teachers as learners, artists and acknowledge them as powerful cultural mediators

The problems besetting the theatre companies are not theirs alone. Teachers are the accomplices of education programs. *Theatre Space* clearly identified the value that teachers place on arts experiences—particularly live theatre—for their students and for themselves. The *Theatre Space* research found that teachers engage with the performances offered by theatre companies for four main reasons—curriculum connections, assessment requirements, content, and to broaden student experience.[47] Earlier research in this area discovered that the teacher's role is critical—they are key cultural mediators. If teachers have to align arts experiences in response to curriculum as well as manage internal school politics and financial constraints, students may see only one performance in their drama studies. 'The one theatre experience that students have is the one that is potentially the benchmark for their relationship to theatre and performance'.[48] We argue for theatre companies to critically consider that the encounter students have with their work is potentially the first and the last. Therefore, it is beholden on them to program work that enables students to experience sophisticated ideas, challenging form, and rich production values.

When we asked teachers why theatre companies should have education programs, their answers were emphatic. Teachers believe that students benefit from them because the programs offer rich learning opportunities outside the traditional classroom. One teacher said, 'I could sit here as an educator and I have a certain bag of tricks but the limitations of that are obvious. You can do some things but not everything.' Having artists re-stating or affirming the 'message' can be very powerful. Significantly, another teacher stated that she wanted to expose her students to a range of different theatre experiences, but that she herself wanted to 'grow' as an educator. 'Educators need to keep educating themselves as artists and have support from theatre companies to do so.' The potential for professional development for teachers as artists is exciting. Several Australian theatre companies offer rich opportunities for teachers to develop their skills and understanding of Shakespeare, stagecraft, direction and acting. There is also space in the landscape for artists as educators, for education and industry to share sector knowledge and reciprocate professional development; a co-valuing of knowledge and practice as opposed to maintaining a master/apprentice model.

We also asked teachers a 'what if'. What if, in a worst case scenario, there were no education programs, how might that impact? One teacher offered:

> *If there were no education programs, I could still take students to the theatre; but what I love about education programs in theatre companies is that they offer experiential learning; students learn through doing and it emphasises their emotional engagement in the form.*

This statement clearly articulates the pedagogical value of education programs, but it also points to the potential of audience building. Radbourne and her colleagues state that audiences 'are active participants who seek out work that increases their knowledge, provides risk, is authentic and offers collective engagement'. In other words today's active participants make tomorrow's informed audiences.

5. Reconsider the power of space

Theatre companies possess a number of powerful resources. One is that they are in the business of live experience and interaction. Live interaction, in our highly digitalized society— the lived experience— provides a unique point of difference, and a clear moment in time. A second powerful resource is the buildings and spaces theatre companies inhabit. Delivering programs in schools supports access, equity and inclusion but in-house theatre education programs are, as Helen Nicholson says, 'symbolic gestures' that say to young people 'you are welcome…along with your backpacks' and that teachers are welcome.[49] Theatre spaces are not classrooms but they are powerful learning environments and in such spaces, important 'contracts' can be made between the participants and the teaching artists. Henri Lefebvre relates the significance of space to the quality of a person's lived experience;[50] and Gaye McCauley states that 'wherever human societies have developed theatre as a mode of expression, they have also constructed building to house it.[51]

As theatre educators and teaching artists we understand the significance of 'space' in the 'contract' that is created during a workshop between students and artists in that space. While McCauley argues that certain cultural centres such as theatre buildings can appear intimidating to some, we argue that excursions enable the breaking down of barriers in perceived adults-only, professional environments. Our experience is that when young people have the opportunity to work and perform inside theatre company spaces it significantly transforms their learning. Enabling young people and teachers to feel welcome by providing genuine access to the various spaces in the building is a powerful pedagogical tool. We support in-school program delivery and its capacity to provide access and engagement, but we champion in-house education program delivery that affords young people a different privilege and a regard that they deserve. Theatre company spaces when offered willingly and purposefully help turn a 'space' into a 'place to be' for young people.

G. Translate and understand the other's language

A major hindrance, as has been clearly illustrated elsewhere in this paper, is the misunderstanding between theatres and educators that can arise from poor understanding of each other's motives and language. Educational discourse, particularly curriculum discourse, is intentionally created for the education sector. Even the terminology of arts-based subjects such as Drama or Theatre Studies—although drawing from industry and theatre language—is created for school-based teaching and assessment. Many education managers will have had to activate their translation skills when educational discourse and theatre language occupy the same space. Most noticeably such disjunctions occur during pre- or post-show discussion forums when the requirements of assessment tasks become evident in student and teacher questions and responses. The specificity of such questions can often lead to an awkward pause, at worst a dismissive response from an artist. The language of curricula can appear cumbersome and even antithetical to the theatre-making process. To be fair, it is a language constructed to enable a shared understanding across a broad range of educational contexts, and must be accepted as such. Similarly, we must accept that the language of theatre is better at defining meaning and process than outcomes.

We argue that the way forward is one of full company collaboration. It is nonsensical to program a student forum, pre- or post-show, unless the artists present are aware of the context, and understand why the students are attending. The act of programming 'schools' performances or programming for an education season is predicated on the fact that schools are attending for educational and possibly study purposes. So theatre companies need to do their homework and educate all those involved in the forum process. Teachers have an important role to play here as well; preparing their students thoroughly, or providing provocations that generate curiosity for students to direct their own learning about the performance they are going to see. Many teachers do but our experience is also that many don't. The discussion earlier on Jane Harrison's *Stolen* is a case in point.

The facilitation of forums and question-and-answer sessions requires the sharing or interpretation of languages but also the active learning of each other's discourse. Collaborative conversations that seek to develop such understanding between the company, creative team and education sector can only support and enhance young people's learning, and ongoing quality program delivery.

7. Break open the gatekeeping

The close relationship that arts education programs inevitably have with curriculum demands consideration of the accompanying gatekeeping. Of course, some theatre companies may explicitly buy into the gatekeeping and offer performances and education program content accordingly. The increase in storybook adaptations for the stage in the past five years certainly suggests this;[52] and this paper has offered several instances where gatekeeping and student experience have come into conflict.

In a recent essay for *Australian Plays*, award-winning playwright Angela Betzien described gatekeepers as those 'experts' who so often regulate the arts experiences of young people.[53] Gatekeepers may be curriculum authorities, teachers or parents. They may be policy makers, producers, programmers or curators—all those who decide what is appropriate for young people to see and study. Betzien argues, and we agree, that when we attempt to protect young people from difficult, different or upsetting things, we risk raising a generation of young people lacking in resilience and the protective skills that will help them to endure pain and crisis in their lives. Maxine Greene believes that young people today are often called upon to make the kinds of choices that their elders seldom had to confront:

> *the use of drugs; birth control and the problem of abortion; decisions with regard to handguns; the predicament of foster children or abandoned children; child abuse; the disintegration of numerous families...Schools of the future, no matter what their origin or allegiance, will be called upon to do more than what is loosely called 'community*

> *service'. Young people need to be coached, at the very least, in the skills required to cope with... [these] complexities.*[54]

It is a compelling argument and an open invitation for theatre companies and schools to partner and enable difficult and challenging conversations.

State curriculum bodies are subject to public critique and potentially to media focus. If a text that is set for study generates controversy or if an examination paper offers a perceivably contentious question, curriculum authorities are accountable; this can perpetuate a gate-keeping approach in selecting literature and play texts. Teachers have to contend with conflicting agendas, those that traverse the expectations of schools and broader community, and the nature and purpose of art. Schools have to account for a diverse range of community and cultural interests and the need to administer their duty of care to all students. Further, individual teachers bring their own tastes and values to their teaching and so to the choices of arts experiences their students will have. Within these complexities and constraints, theatre companies and educators need to be pre-emptive.

The Australian Curriculum clearly states that Critical and Creative Thinking, Intercultural Understanding, Ethical Understanding and Personal and Social Capability are key pillars of a young Australian's learning. Further, it states that the role of the Arts is 'to entertain, challenge, provoke responses and enrich our knowledge of self, communities, world cultures and histories' and that 'the Arts contribute to the development of confident and creative individuals, nurturing and challenging active and informed citizens'. The challenges of increasingly complex communities invite theatre companies to boldly program powerful and risky work that opens up conversations and generates interventions so that students and teachers can tackle big questions and relevant issues in a shared and supportive environment. It is worth reminding the gatekeepers that theirs is a mutually reliant partnership. It is time the various curriculum authorities looked to industry as equal partners in learning.

At the International Teaching Artists Conference in Brisbane, July 2014, two statements resonated.[55] Scott Rankin from *biG hART* repeatedly stated in his keynote that the world cannot always be viewed through western eyes, and Jade Lillie, CEO of Footscray Community Arts Centre, challenged the delegates to consider who is doing the teaching and who is doing the learning in any arts encounter. Young people cannot feel empowered or enabled to make decisions unless they can contribute meaningfully to and shape the experiences that they have. They need to be asked and they need to be listened to, in order to 'have a sense of optimism about their lives and the future'.[56] Theatre has an important role to play here. It can pose critical questions, offer a world view that recognises difficult experiences, and theatre companies can work closely with educators to enable young people to develop a sense of optimism. Jonothan Neelands argues 'Drama and Theatre is the quintessential social artform and this quality is also essential to its educational uses. People must come together in order to make and to share in its makings. It is the art of togetherness'.[57]

8. Train education managers as arts and creative industry professionals

Theatre company education managers are highly skilled. As experienced contenders in this field we argue that to be an education manager you need to have or acquire the following:

- a strong desire to work with young people and educators;
- good inter-personal (read inter-departmental) communication skills; meeting skills; producing, curatorial and programming skills;
- an understanding of touring management; administrative, ticketing and booking knowledge; budget and finance skills; capacity to understand business models; strategic planning;
- a knowledge of contemporary theatre making practice; a knowledge of historical theatre practice;
- directorial skills;
- detailed knowledge of state and federal curriculum across several learning areas;
- knowledge of a range of education contexts including operational

procedures, school finance systems, term dates and key assessment periods;

- teaching skills; facilitation skills; knowledge of a range of arts based pedagogies;
- resource writing skills; workshop planning;
- funding and grant writing skills;
- an acute understanding of the language of education and the language of contemporary theatre practice; translating skills;
- skill in diplomacy.

It is a daunting position description yet it is the lived reality of many education managers and the experience of workplace demands/opportunities that we have encountered in the field. We have moved on from the stridency of advocating for our department—why does no-one see that theatre and education are important?—and know that Education Managers (with capital letters) are serious contributors to the industry's viability. We propose an arts leadership model that trains education managers as cultural leaders, one that requires companies to seriously invest in and recognise their leadership

The MPAG Education Forum in Brisbane in 2014 offered two presentations that strongly supported the concept of training education managers as significant arts and cultural leaders. David Sudmalis from Community Partnerships, Australia Council, strongly advocated broad community engagement in order to market programs, augment or build the audience base, create more fruitful relationships and a sense of 'co-ownership' of projects. Creative industries consultant, Caroline Sharpen, offered education managers ways to effect powerful internal advocacy, especially for new projects, including knowing the company's planning cycle, always considering an all-of organisation-point of view, proposing a careful budget, and building a strong business case.[58]

Organisationally, these and the extensive qualifications list are important intersection points for education programs both within companies and across the theatre and education sectors. We propose a model that trains education managers as cultural leaders, one that requires companies to seriously invest in and recognise such leadership and the contribution it makes to the company. We urge every theatre company and their management to realistically consider and advocate for such a model.

9. Build a legacy

> *So the 'why' of why we should do it is because that's what cultural organisations are set up to do. All arts organisations should be involved in running participation programs because contemporary life demands that we do this. We are all involved in the process of continuous learning.*[59]

The questions that theatre companies might also like to ask themselves is what will they leave behind? Is it a digital archive of showreels and promos that will find its way some day to a central curated repository? Education programs, well resourced, valued and powerfully positioned within an organisation offer the opportunity to leave a living breathing legacy of theatre-making practice and critical thinking in the young people they engage with in respectful and meaningful ways. It is time that the reality reflected the rhetoric.

Every business or corporation with any aspiration of surviving our rapidly changing world has a research and development program, an area inside their organisation that looks at the current world, their current product and potential markets to expand those markets, to develop new and exciting products and forms. Education programs offer theatre companies this very capacity. The analogue nature of theatre is, in a time of rapid digital engagement, fresh and innovative because of that.

Our major theatre companies are often criticised for their lack of diversity in both their programming and their artists, for reflecting primarily a white middle-class society. This is the current demographic of the subscriber. An education program, on the other hand, brings students from a wider range of cultural and financial backgrounds, many of whom would not access the arts through their families or through other means. The backpacks in the foyer belong to a more accurate representation of contemporary Australia than the slice represented by subscription holders. Any theatre company that wants to assert their relevance to contemporary Australian culture, to nurture a more diverse group of artists and audiences, to discover new stories and ways of telling them, will find it an astute move to rethink and regenerate their education programs, develop new work for this constituency, engage in rich conversations with students and their teachers and build longevity in their relationships with their valued team. Education and theatre is indeed an act of togetherness.

THE AUSTRALIAN CURRICULUM—THE ARTS: A POSTSCRIPT

20 September 2014

As this publication goes to print rumours abound about the Donnelly-Wiltshire review of the Australian Curriculum. Reportedly there is disagreement between the two reviewers and influential input from some state curriculum authorities. What is of concern is the growing sense that arts education for Australian children will become 'optional' as opposed to mandated. A key recommendation currently being made is to pare back the national curriculum, which would give primary focus to 'basic skills like literary and numeracy'. Should the arts' value be diminished and lose status in the written curriculum, theatre companies will have a critical role to play in arts education for young Australians. There is an urgency here that cannot be ignored.

Endnotes

1. *Creative Australia*, National Cultural Policy 2013, p.77, http://creativeaustralia.arts.gov.au/assets/Creative-Australia-PDF-20130417.pdf (accessed July 2014).
2. Australian Government Department of Education, *Review of the Australian Curriculum,* http://www.studentsfirst.gov.au/review-australian-curriculum (accessed September, 2014).
3. Ben Eltham, 'Australia Council confirms: Creative Australia is Dead', *Arts Hub*, Friday 2 August, 2014, http://www.artshub.com.au/news-article/features/all-arts/australia-council-confirms-creative-australia-is-dead-24549 (accessed September, 2014).
4. Simon Darcy and Bronwen Dalton, 'We need ABS arts and sports data to understand our culture', *The Conversation*, 1 August, 2014, http://theconversation.com/we-need-abs-arts-and-sports-data-to-understand-our-culture-3025 (accessed September, 2014).
5. UNESCO, Road Map for Arts Education, 2006, www.unesco.org/new/fileadmin/MULTIMEDIA/HQ/CLT/CLT/pdf/Arts_Edu_RoadMap_en.pdf.
6. ACARA—*The Australian Curriculum—the Arts* http://www.australiancurriculum.edu.au/the-arts/introductionhttp://www.australiancurriculum.edu.au/the-arts/introduction (accessed September, 2014).
7. Sonia Bahri, 'Educating Through Art in Secondary Education', *Education through Art: Building Partnerships for Secondary Education* (Proceedings) UNESCO, 2005, p.4, http://unesdoc.unesco.org/images/0014/001442/144239e.pdf.
8. Edward B. Fiske (ed.) *Champions of Change: The Impact of Arts on Learning*, p ixx, http://artsedge.kennedy-ecenter.org/champions/pdfs/ChampsReport.pdf.
9. Wendy Schiller, 'Children's perceptions of live arts performance: A longitudinal study', *Early Child Development and Care,* No. 175, 2005, http://www.tandfonline.com/doi/abs/10.1080/030044305001314111?journalCode=gecd20#preview.
10. Robert Ewing, 'The Arts and Australian Education: Realising potential', *Australian Education Review,* Australian Council for

Educational Research (ACER) 2010, http://research.acer.edu.au/aer/11/.

11. John O'Toole, R-J Adams, M. Anderson, B. Burton and Robert Ewing (Ed) *Young Audiences, Theatre and the Cultural Conversation*, Springer Publications 2013, //www.springer.com/education+%26+language/book/978-94-007-7608-1.
12. Meg Upton was a Lead Research Assistant on the Theatre Space Project 2009–1 working on four case studies with the University of Melbourne, including Declan Greene's *Moth.*
13. *The Role of Arts Education in Academic Motivation, Engagement and Achievement*, Australia Council/ University of Sydney, 2013, http://www.australiacouncil.gov.au/research-hub/arts_rippa/arts_rippa_projects/the_role_of_arts_education_in_academic_motivation,_engagement,_and_achievement (assessed September 2014).
14. NAPLAN http://www.nap.edu.au/naplan/naplan.html.
15. The MacArthur Foundation, *Connected Learning* http://www.macfound.org/press/from-field/website-connected-learning/ (accessed September, 2014).
16. Arts Victoria, Arts and Education Mapping Project Questionnaire 2007, http://www.arts.vic.gov.au/Research_Resources/Research_Program.
17. Geoffrey Milne, *Theatre Australia (Un)limited: Australian Theatre Since the 1950s,* Sydney: Angus and Robertson, 2004; Kathleen Gallagher and David Booth (eds) *How Theatre Educates: Convergences and Counterpoints,* University of Toronto Press, 2003; Anthony Jackson, *Theatre, Education and the Making of Meanings: Art or Instrument*? Manchester University Press, 2007; John O'Toole, John Stinson and Madonna Moore, *Drama and Curriculum: A Giant at the Door,* Springer, 2009; Helen Nicholson, *Theatre and Education*, London: Palgrave MacMillan, 2009.
18. Drawn directly from current theatre company websites (accessed August 2014).
19. From http://www.education.gov.au/schooling (accessed September 2014).
20. Clare Watson left Malthouse in early 201 to take up the role of Director in Residence at the Malthouse and has subsequently been appointed as Artistic Director of St Martin's Youth Theatre in Melbourne.
21. Declan Greene, *Moth and Home Economics.* Sydney: Currency Press 2012.
22. Arena Theatre Company is a Melbourne based theatre company

established in 1966, making work for young people between the ages of and 2 http://www.arenatheatre.com.au/.

23. Chris Kohn and Meg Upton, *Challenging Theatre for Young Audiences*, co-presentation, Drama Victoria Conference 2010.
24. Australia Council for the Arts, *Anticipating Change in the Major Performing Arts* report, 2008, http://www.australiacouncil.gov.au/__data/assets/pdf_file/0010/35596/Anticipating_change.pdf p.25.
25. Australia Council Report - *More than Bums on Seats,* 2008. http://www.australiacouncil.gov.au/__data/assets/pdf_file/0004/71257/Full_report_More_than_bums_on_seats_Australian_participation_in_the_arts2.pdf.
26. Jennifer Radbourne, Katya Johanson, Hilary Glow and Tabitha White, 'The Audience Experience: Measuring Quality in the Performing Arts' in *International Journal of Arts Management*, Spring 2009, 11:3, pp.16–29.
27. *Theatre Space* Final Report, 2012, p.98, now published as *Young Audiences, Theatre and the Cultural Conversation*, Springer 2013.
28. Memorandum to Artistic/Management, Playbox/Malthouse, 2005. In the author's possession.
29. *Anticipating Change in the Major Performing Arts* Report, Australia Council, 2008, p.24.
30. Memo to Artistic Management, Malthouse Theatre, September 2005. In the author's possession,
31. From Playbox Education School Attendance figures 2000–2004.
32. From Playbox Education School Attendance figures 2000–2004.
33. The 201 VCE Playlist application process was posted at http://www.rav.net.au/news/creative-communities/nominations-for-the-2015-vce-drama-and-theatre-studies-play-lists-are-now-open (accessed June 2014),
34. Johanna Wyn and Rob White, *Rethinking Youth*, London: Sage Publications 1997; Peter Dwyer and Johanna Wyn, *Youth, Education and Risk: Facing the Future*, London: Routledge, 2004.
35. Jane Kroger, *Identity in adolescence: The balance between self and other*, London: Routledge, 198 p.1.
36. Phyllis R. Magrab, *The Adolescent Learner and the Aesthetic Experience: A Brief Overview,* Education through Art: Building Partnerships in Secondary Education, UNESCO Expert Panel Meeting 200 (Published Proceedings, 2006), pp.7–11, http://unesdoc.unesco.org/images/0014/001442/144239e.pdf.
37. Suzie Thomas has been Education Manager at the Melbourne Theatre Company since 2009. She was interviewed by Meg Upton in early 2013.

38. *I Love you Bro* by Adam Cass, for more information see: http://www.playlab.org.au/index.php/publications/shop/i-love-you-bro-by-adam-j-a-cass-detail.
39. The Malthouse Theatre education staff were interviewed in mid-201 by Meg Upton.
40. Australian Major Performing Arts Group—Education http://www.ampag.com.au/education.htm.
41. Company Meeting, Monday 1 May 2005, Playbox Theatre Company. In the author's possession.
42. *Creative Australia* http://creativeaustralia.arts.gov.au/assets/Creative-Australia-PDF-20130417.pdf p.77.
43. Interview with Education Team from the Young Vic, London, July 2013.
44. The authors visited and spoke to education staff at the National Theatre, the Lincoln Centre and the Young Vic at various times during 201 and 2013. Education staff from the Tate Modern presented at the International Teaching Artists' Conference in Brisbane in July 2014.
45. The Australian Curriculum (v7.0) The Arts, http://www.australiancurriculum.edu.au/the-arts/rationale
46. Radbourne Glow, Johanson *The Audience Experience.*
47. *Theatre Space* (2012) Final Report, p.9 (now published as John O'Toole et al, *Young Audiences, Theatre and the Cultural Conversation*).
48. Meg Upton, 'Articulating the Theatre Experience: Frames of Response', *Drama Australia Journal* NJ, Volume 33, Number 2, 201 p.59.
49. Helen Nicholson, *Theatre and Education*, London: Palgrave Macmillan 2009, p.59.
50. Henri Lefebvre, *The Production of Space*, London: Blackwell 1984.
51. McAuley G (2008) *Space in Performance: Making Meaning in the Theatre*, Ann Arbor: University of Michigan Press, p.36.
52. Elissa Blake, 'Children's Theatre Companies play it by the book in bid to lure families', *Sydney Morning Herald,* 1 April, 2014, http://www.smh.com.au/entertainment/theatre/childrens-theatre-companies-play-it-by-the-book-in-bid-to-lure-families-20140411-36il9.html (accessed September, 2014).
53. Angela Betzian, 'Writing in the Dark', *AustralianPlays.org*, http://australianplays.org/writing-in-the-dark (accessed 1 September, 2014).
54. Maxine Greene M, 'Imaging Futures: The public school and possibility', *Journal of Curriculum Studies*, Vol. 32, Issue 2,

Taylor & Francis online, 2010, http://www.tandfonline.com/doi/abs/10.1080/002202700182754#.VBgCQPmSzl4.

55. Second International Teaching Artists Conference, QUT, Brisbane, July 2014.
56. The Melbourne Declaration, 2008, http://www.curriculum.edu.au/verve/_resources/National_Declaration_on_the_Educational_Goals_for_Young_Australians.pdf.
57. Jonothan Neelands, 'The Art of Togetherness: Reflections on some essential artistic and pedagogic qualities of drama curricula', *Drama Australia Journal,* NJ, 2009, Vol.1, No.1, p.15.
58. Personal notes from The MPAG Education Managers Forum, Brisbane 2014.
59. Robin Penty, former Head of Participation at Arts Centre Melbourne, was interviewed by Naomi Edwards and Meg Upton in March, 2013.

FORTHCOMING

PP40, February 2015
EDUCATION AND THE ARTS:\
Creativity in the promised new order
Meg Upton with Naomi Edwards

Musicals are big business and Australians perform them well. It is estimated that Andrew Lloyd Webber's *The Phantom of the Opera* has been seen by more than 130 million people globally, and the total worldwide gross is now in excess of $5.6 billion. In Australia the remount budget for *Wicked* was in excess of $12 million, but it played to 1.4 million patrons earning $125 million in ticket sales. For the Australia Council, however, the investment risk has been too high and too risky: a problem best left to the commercial arena.

We need a strategic, professionally charted Australian music theatre matrix; a creative development process that brings producers, new work, investors, venues and audience together. Julian Meyrick argues for a National Theatre to preserve and encourage investment in local drama. Similarly we need to argue for infrastructure and funding to develop the music theatre sector and tell our musical stories, develop our cultural tourism and pursue the global market.

Copyright Information

PLATFORM PAPERS
Quarterly essays from Currency House Inc.
Founding Editor: Dr John Golder
Currency House is a not-for-profit association and resource centre advocating the role of the performing arts in public life by research, debate and publication.

Postal address: PO Box 2270, Strawberry Hills, NSW 2012, Australia
Email: info@currencyhouse.org.au Tel: (02) 9319 4953
Website: www.currencyhouse.org.au Fax: (02) 9319 3649

ISBN 978-0-9924890-2-1
ISSN 1449-583X

Typeset in Garamond
Printed by McPhersons
Production by Xou Creative